A
Cheever
Evening

A Cheever Evening

A New Play Based on Stories of John Cheever
by A.R. Gurney

Playwrights Horizons, Inc.
New York City, produced
the World Premiere of
A Cheever Evening Off-Broadway
in 1994.

GARDEN CITY, NEW YORK

All inquiries concerning English language stock and non-
professional stage preforming rights in the United States
and Canada should be directed to Dramatists Play Service, Inc., 440 Park Avenue South, New York, N.Y. 10016.

Inquiries concerning all other rights should be addressed
to William Morris Agency, Inc., 1325 Avenue of the
Americas, New York, N.Y. 10019, Attn: Gilbert Parker.

Photos of the 1994 Off-Broadway production by
T. Charles Erickson.

Design by Maria Chiarino

ISBN 1-56865-135-X

MANUFACTURED IN THE UNITED STATES OF AMERICA

A **Cheever Evening** opened at Playwrights Horizons on October 6, 1994. It was directed by Don Scardino. The set was designed by John Lee Beatty, the costumes by Jennifer Von Mayrhauser, the lighting by Kenneth Posner and the sound by Aural Fixation. The Casting Director was Janet Foster, the Production Manager, Jack O'Connor and the Production Stage Manager Lloyd Davis, Jr.

The ensemble in alphabetical order:

John Cunningham
Jack Gilpin
Julie Hagerty
Mary Beth Peil
Robert Stanton
Jennifer Van Dyck

Time: The late Forties to the early Seventies

Place: The east side of Manhattan. The northern suburbs. The New England Coast.

To
Don Scardino

CAST

A minimum of six: three men, three women. The distribution of roles is indicated in the script. Parts have been assigned to reflect equality, fluidity and versatility.

COSTUMES

Simple, basic suits or dresses with minor accessories added as needed. There might be some attention to changing styles as the play moves from the late Forties through the Fifties and Sixties into the early Seventies.

PROPS AND ACCESSORIES

Only what is essential.

SET

A number of pieces of good, simple, Early American furniture, set against backgrounds which invoke, first, a Manhattan skyline, then a Westchester backyard and finally a seascape. The furniture should look inherited, the kind that might belong in any of these locales. For example, a couch, a schoolbench, a table and several Windsor chairs. A dry sink may be used as a bar and as a source and repository for props and accessories.

LIGHTING

Interiors and exteriors. Light is essential in Cheever. We should move from the yellow, slanting light of New York to the lush green foliage of the suburbs on to the gray-blue sky of the seashore.

SOUND

Music from the Fifties and Sixties. Other sounds as indicated.

(This play may also be presented simply as a reading, with actors using stools and music stands.)

NOTE FROM THE PLAYWRIGHT: Over the years, I have adapted several John Cheever short stories for the stage or television. Here I have tried to shape a more complicated tapestry by interweaving elements from a sizeable number of his works. Wherever possible, I have used Cheever's language and events, but I also have made changes to accommodate the special demands of the stage. What I hope to do is pay homage to a major American author and a major influence on my own writing.

Act One ———

ACT ONE

AT RISE: *A party is in progress. Lush Fifties music in the background, say, the Harry James recording of "You'll Never Know." Everyone is onstage. First Actor is making First Actress a drink. Second Actor and Second Actress are conversing and smoking. Third Actor and Third Actress are dancing an easy foxtrot. All are talking animatedly. The music modulates to a Benny Goodman quartet as the actors come downstage to address the audience.*

FIRST ACTOR (*as if bringing us into the party*): We are talking of a time when the city of New York was filled with a river light . . .

FIRST ACTRESS: And when you heard the Benny Goodman quartets from a radio in the corner stationery store . . .

SECOND ACTOR: And almost everybody wore a hat . . .

SECOND ACTRESS (*putting out her cigarette*): We are the last of that generation of chain smokers who woke the world in the morning with their coughing . . .

THIRD ACTOR: Who sailed for Europe on ships . . .

THIRD ACTRESS: Who were truly nostalgic for love and happiness . . .

SECOND ACTRESS: And whose gods were as ancient as yours, whoever you are.

FIRST ACTOR: It was long ago . . .

FIRST ACTRESS: So long ago that the foliage of elm trees was part of the summer night . . .

THIRD ACTOR: So long ago that when you wanted to make a left turn, you cranked down the car window and *pointed* in that direction . . .

THIRD ACTRESS: Otherwise you were not allowed to point.

SECOND ACTOR: "Don't point," you were told.

SECOND ACTRESS: I can't imagine why.

FIRST ACTOR (*affectionately*): Maybe the gesture was thought to be erotic.

FIRST ACTRESS (*taking his arm*): And maybe it was . . .

(*First Actor and Actress withdraw upstage with the Third Actor and Third Actress. The Second Actor and Second Actress remain downstage. They become Jim and Irene*)

JIM (*to audience; arm around Irene*): Jim and Irene Westcott were the kind of people who seem to strike that satisfactory average of income, endeavor and respectability that is reached by the statistical reports in college alumni bulletins.

IRENE (*to audience*): They were the parents of two young children, had been married nine years and lived on the twelfth floor of an apartment house near Sutton Place.

JIM: They went to the theatre on an average of 10.3 times a year . . .

IRENE: That much?

JIM: According to the statistics.

IRENE: And they hoped someday to live up in Westchester County . . .

JIM (*settling into a chair*): They differed from their neighbors only in an interest they shared in serious music . . .

IRENE (*turning on a "radio," which might be suggested by a patch of light downstage*): They had a new Magnavox console radio, and they spent a good deal of time listening to music on it.

(*She settles down with her needlepoint. A Chopin prelude is heard; they listen, then*)

FIRST ACTOR (*behind them, slamming his hand on the "keyboard"*): For Chrissake, Kathy, do you always have to play the piano when I get home?

FIRST ACTRESS (*behind them*): It's the only chance I have. I'm at the office all day.

FIRST ACTOR: So am I! Which makes it hell to come home to that shitty piano!

(*Sound of a door slamming. The Chopin resumes. Pause*)

IRENE (*to Jim*): Did you hear that?

JIM: I did.

IRENE: On the *radio?*

JIM: I heard.

IRENE: The man said something dirty.

JIM: It's probably a play.

IRENE: It didn't sound like a play . . . try another station.

(*Jim gets up and turns a "dial"*)

THIRD ACTOR (*behind them*): Have you seen my garters?

THIRD ACTRESS (*behind them*): Button me up.

THIRD ACTOR: I said, have you seen my garters?

THIRD ACTRESS: Just button me up and I'll find your garters.

THIRD ACTOR: I wish you wouldn't leave apple cores in the ashtrays. I hate the smell.

(*Another pause*)

JIM: Strange, isn't it?

IRENE: Isn't it?

(*Jim turns the "dial" again*)

FIRST ACTRESS (*singing in an English accent; rocking a "baby"*):
"Trot, trot, trot to Boston,
Trot, trot, trot to Lynn!"

IRENE: My God! That's the Sweeney's nurse, in 17-B!

FIRST ACTRESS:
"Trot, trot, trot to Salem,
And then come home again . . ."

IRENE: Turn that thing off!

JIM: Why?

IRENE: Maybe they can hear *us!* (*Jim turns it off*) We must be getting other people's apartments.

JIM: Impossible.

IRENE: But that was the Sweeney's nurse! She sings that song in the elevator!

JIM: Let me try it again. (*Jim turns on "radio" again*)

FIRST ACTRESS (*singing*): "Ride a cock horse to Banbury cross . . ."

IRENE: There she is again!

JIM (*into "radio"*): Hello? . . . Hello? . . . (*To Irene*) They can't hear us.

IRENE: Then try something else.

(*Jim turns the "dial." The others sing "The Whiffenpoof Song"*)

THIRD ACTRESS: Eat some more sandwiches!

(*Others sing exuberantly underneath*)

IRENE (*joining Jim by the "radio"*): That's the Fuller's in 11-E.

JIM: No.

IRENE: That's the Fullers! She was in the liquor store this afternoon, planning a party tonight.

JIM: Why weren't we invited?

IRENE: Because we don't *know* them, Jim.

JIM: Maybe we will now.

IRENE: See if you can get those peculiar people in 18-C.

JIM (*to audience, as he fiddles with the "dial"*): And so that night we heard a monologue on salmon fishing in Canada, and a bridge game, and later on . . .

FIRST ACTOR: What's the matter, honey?

FIRST ACTRESS: I can't sleep.

FIRST ACTOR: Do you feel all right?

FIRST ACTRESS: I don't really feel like myself. there are only fifteen or twenty minutes in the week when I feel like myself.

FIRST ACTOR: We'll try another doctor tomorrow.

FIRST ACTRESS: Oh these doctors. These *bills* . . . (*They go off*)

(*Jim and Irene look at each other*)

JIM (*turning off the "radio"*): Maybe we should go to bed.

IRENE: Maybe we should.

JIM (*to audience*): But the next evening, when I came home . . .

IRENE: Quickly! Go up to 16-C, Jim! Mr. Osborne's beating his wife! They've been quarreling since four o'clock!

JIM: I can't just—

IRENE (*turning on the "radio"*): But he's hurting her! Listen! (*They listen. Sounds of bedsprings and lovemaking. They look at each other*) Well now it's stopped.

JIM (*turning it off*): Have you been listening all *day?*

IRENE: Of course not! (*Pause*) Just occasionally. (*Pause*) It's been horrible. Mrs. Melville's mother died, and some woman is having an affair with the handyman, and that girl who walks the poodle is a whore.

JIM: Irene . . .

IRENE: What?

JIM: I spent a great deal of money on that radio. I bought it to give you some pleasure.

IRENE: You bought it for yourself too, Jim.

JIM: I bought it mainly for you. I'm not here all day.

IRENE: You seem to be blaming me for something.

JIM: Not blaming. Just pointing out a simple fact.

IRENE: Don't, don't, DON'T quarrel with me, Jimmy, please. Everybody in the world has been quarreling, all day long.

JIM: Then don't listen.

IRENE: I won't. I'm trying not to. (*They look at the "radio"*) We've never been like that, have we, darling? I mean we've always been good and decent and loving to one another. We've got two sweet children, and we're happy, aren't we?

JIM: Of course we're happy. I'll have that damned radio fixed first thing. (*To audience*) So I called the store. (*The piano now plays Debussy's "La Mer." Jim turns to Irene*) Better?

IRENE (*somewhat disappointedly*): Oh yes. The man came, and it's been fine ever since.

JIM: I saw the repair bill on the hall table. Four hundred dollars.

IRENE: Apparently it required some major adjustment.

JIM: That's our last extravagance this year.

IRENE: Let's hope . . .

(*They listen to the music*)

JIM: I also noticed, on the hall table, a bill from Saks.

IRENE: Oh. Yes.

JIM: You haven't paid the Saks bill yet?

IRENE: I'll pay it next month.

JIM: Why did you tell me you'd already paid it?

IRENE: I didn't want you to worry.

JIM: You lied to me.

IRENE: I didn't *lie*, Jim.

JIM: I'm not at all sure of the future, and frankly I don't like to see all my labors wasted in fur coats and slipcovers and expensive radios!

IRENE (*turning off the "radio." The piano stops*): Please, Jim. They'll hear us.

JIM: Who'll hear us?

IRENE: The radio.

JIM: The radio *can't* hear us. Nobody can hear us. (*Shouting*) Nobody in the goddam world can hear us!

IRENE: Oh Jim. Please!

JIM: And what if they *can?* Who gives a shit?

IRENE: Stop it. You know I hate that word.

JIM: Why are you so Christly all of a sudden? What's turned you overnight into a convent girl? You stole your mother's jewelry before they probated her will. You never gave your sister a cent—not even when she needed it. And where was all your piety when you went to that abortionist? I'll never forget how cool you were. You packed your bag and went off to have that child murdered as if you were going to Nassau! Oh hell, I'm getting a drink! (*He goes to the "bar"*)

IRENE (*kneeling by the "radio"*): She thought of the radio, and hoped it might once again speak to her kindly.

JIM (*crossing behind her*): I've worked my ass off for you and the kids! I've broken my back for you guys! (*He goes out*)

IRENE (*to audience*): Maybe she'd hear some Chopin, or at
  least the soothing song of the Sweeney's nurse . . .
  (*Turns on the radio*)

FIRST ACTOR'S VOICE: An early morning railroad disaster in
  Tokyo killed twenty-nine people and injured at least . . .

FIRST ACTRESS'S VOICE (*overlapping*): A fire in a Catholic
  hospital near Buffalo was extinguished early this morning,
  after causing several deaths and thousands of dollars'
  worth of . . .

FIRST ACTOR'S VOICE (*overlapping*): The temperature is forty-
  seven . . .

FIRST ACTRESS: The humidity is eighty-nine . . .

IRENE: But that's all she heard, so she turned it off.

(*She turns off the "radio," as we hear party sounds. Laura
comes on, played by Third Actress*)

LAURA: Is this where we powder our noses?

IRENE (*vaguely*): What? . . . Oh yes . . . feel free . . .
  (*She goes off*)

(*Laura pulls up a chair as if to a dressing table and powders
her nose as if in a mirror. Alice comes on, played by First
Actress*)

ALICE: Hi.

LAURA: Oh hi.

ALICE: Say, could I borrow a splash of perfume? I seem to
  have left mine at home.

LAURA: Certainly. Certainly you can, Alice. (*Hands her a perfume spray*)

ALICE (*looking at it*): Hmmm. *Taboo* . . . how fancy. (*She sprays herself, hands it back*)

LAURA: Ralph gave it to me for Christmas.

ALICE (*now combing her hair*): I hear you've moving to California.

LAURA: We hope so. We'll know tomorrow.

ALICE: Is it a good job?

LAURA: Ralph thinks so.

ALICE: You're lucky.

LAURA: I suppose we are.

ALICE: California . . .

LAURA: It's kind of scary, actually. To pick up stakes.

ALICE: Scary, hell. You're very, very lucky. You don't know how lucky you are. (*Brushing her hair angrily*) I have this cake of soap. I mean, I *had* this cake of soap. Somebody gave it to me when I was married. Some maid, some music teacher. It was good English soap, the kind I like, and I decided to save it for when Larry made a killing and could take me to Bermuda. First, I thought I could use it when he got the job in Hartford. Then, when we went to Boston. And then, when he got work here, I thought maybe this time, maybe *now* I get to take the kids out of public schools and pay the bills and move out of those second-rate rentals we've been living in. Well last week, I was looking through my bureau drawers, and there it was, this cake of soap. It was all cracked, so I threw it out. I threw it out because I knew I never was going to have a chance to use it. I'm never going to Bermuda. I'm never even going to get to Florida. I'll never get out of hock, ever, ever, *ever*. For the rest of my life, for the rest of my *life*, I'll be wearing ragged slips and torn nightgowns and shoes that hurt. And every taxi driver and doorman and headwaiter in this town is going to know in a minute that I haven't got five bucks in this black imitation-suede purse that I've been brushing and brushing and brushing for the past ten years. (*She sits down next to Laura*) How do you rate it, Laura? What's so wonderful about you that you get a break like this? (*She runs her fingers down Laura's arm*) Can I rub it off you? Will that make me lucky? I swear to Jesus, I would murder somebody if I thought it would bring us any money. I'd wring somebody's neck—yours, anybody's—I swear to Jesus I would—! (*She stops herself*) Well anyway. Thanks for the *Taboo*.

(*She hurries off. Laura becomes Betsy as she ties on an apron and sets two silver candlesticks on the table. Bob comes on, wearing a hat, carrying a briefcase. He is played by Third Actor. He scuffs his feet*)

BOB (*to audience, tossing off his hat*): Betsy and I both come from that enormous stratum of the middle class that is distinguished by its ability to recall better times. Lost money is so much a part of our lives that I am sometimes reminded of a group of expatriots, who have adapted themselves energetically to some alien soil, but who are reminded, now and then, of the escarpments of their native coast. (*Betsy has gone to a "window" downstage, and stands staring out*) I'm home! (*He kisses her on the cheek; she continues to stare out*) Sometimes my wife stands in the middle of the room, as if she had lost or forgotten something, and this moment of reflection is so deep that she will not hear me if I speak to her, or the children if they call. (*He puts down his briefcase*) Is it O.K. if the kids listen to *The Lone Ranger*? (*No response*) Do I smell corned beef hash on the stove? Mmmmm. Yummy. (*No response*) Want me to light the candles? (*Still no response; he takes some bills from his briefcase, goes to the table, starts to work*)

BETSY (*finally*): Do you remember the Trenchers?

BOB: The Trenchers?

BETSY: We met them last month at the Newsome's. He's a doctor. She's older. Talks constantly about her dog.

BOB: Oh right.

BETSY: He's there.

BOB: Where?

BETSY (*indicating*): Down there. On the street.

BOB: Trencher?

BETSY: Come here and see.

BOB (*coming to the window, looking out*): Ah. Walking the dog.

BETSY: He wasn't walking the dog when I first looked out. He was just standing there, staring up at this building.

BOB: This *building*?

BETSY: That's what he says he does. He says he comes over here and stares up at our lighted windows.

BOB: When did he say this?

BETSY: At the playground.

BOB: At the *play*ground?

BETSY: He stands outside the gate and stares at me. Yesterday he walked me home. That's when he made his declaration.

BOB: What declaration?

BETSY: He said he loves me. He can't live without me. He'd walk through fire to hear the notes of my voice. (*She laughs*) That's what he said.

BOB: You'd better go to another playground.

BETSY: I did. But he followed me there. . . . Oh I know he's crazy, darling, but I feel so sorry for him. He says that he's never compromised in his life and he's not going to compromise about this.

BOB: What does that mean?

BETSY: I'm not sure. . . . Well, I'll get dinner. (*She goes off*)

BOB (*to audience as he returns to working on his bills*): I was tired that night, and worried about taxes and bills, and I could think of Trencher's "declaration" only as a comical mistake. I felt that he, like every other man I knew, was a captive of financial and sentimental commitments. He was no more free to fall in love with a strange woman he met at some party than he was to take a walking trip through French Guiana . . . (*The telephone rings; Bob answers*) Yes? . . . Hello? . . . Who is this? (*He slams down the phone*) Then I wondered if it might be more serious. In his helplessness, Trencher might have touched that wayward passion my wife shares with some women —that inability to refuse any cry for help. It is not a reasonable passion, and I would almost rather have had her desire him than pity him. (*The telephone rings again; he answers*) Hello? . . . Lookit, I know it's you, Trencher! . . . It's late, we are trying to have dinner, so get off the line, you creep, or I'll call the cops! (*Slams down the phone. To audience*) And that seemed to work. But then the kids got sick.

(*Betsy crosses the stage with a tray; her shoes are off*)

BETSY (*to audience*): I had to deal with them all day . . . (*She goes off*)

BOB (*to audience*): We took turns getting up at night. And I often fell asleep at my desk . . .

BETSY (*coming back on, carrying a vase of roses*): As did I, in my chair, after dinner . . .

(*She puts the flowers on a table, fusses with them*)

BOB: What are those?

BETSY: What do they look like?

BOB: Don't get wise, Betsy. I'm too tired.

BETSY: They arrived this afternoon. I just haven't had time to deal with them.

BOB: From your mother?

BETSY: From Trencher.

BOB: Oh Christ.

BETSY: He said they were to cheer me up.

BOB: He *said?*

BETSY: He brought them to the door.

BOB: Oh Jesus, Betsy.

BETSY: I didn't let him in, Bob.

BOB (*taking the vase*): Out they go, down the incinerator.

BETSY: Don't you dare!

BOB: Now! (*He starts off*)

BETSY: Bob! (*He stops*) Do you realize I haven't been out of this apartment in two weeks?

BOB: It hasn't been quite two weeks.

BETSY: It's been *over* two weeks.

BOB: Well, let's figure it out. The children got sick on a Saturday, which was the 4th—

BETSY: Stop it, Bob! Just *stop* it! I know how long it's been. I haven't had my shoes on in two weeks.

BOB: It could be worse.

BETSY: My mother's cooks had a better life.

BOB: I doubt that.

BETSY (*taking off her apron; throwing it onto a chair*): My mother's cooks had a better *life!* They had pleasant rooms. No one could come into the kitchen without their permission. They had days *off!*

BOB: How long was he here this afternoon?

BETSY: A minute. I told you.

BOB: He got *in?* He *stayed?*

BETSY: No. I did not let him in! And you know why? Because I looked so terrible. I didn't want to discourage him.

BOB: Oh God!

BETSY: He makes me feel marvelous. The things he tells me make me feel marvelous!

BOB: I don't believe this! (*A tapping sound from above*) What's that?

BETSY: That? I'll tell you what that is. That is the people upstairs, tapping on the radiator! That is our fellow prisoners in our common penitentiary, signaling through the plumbing! That's what that is!

BOB: Do you want to go?

BETSY: Go?

BOB: Leave.

BETSY: Where would I go? Dobbs Ferry? Mount Kisco?

BOB: I mean with Trencher.

BETSY: I don't know, Bob. I don't *know*. What harm would
it do if I did? Is divorce so dreadful? Is marriage the most
wonderful thing in the world? When I was at school in
France, I wrote a long paper on Flaubert in French. A
professor from the University of Chicago wrote me a letter. Today I couldn't read a French *news*paper without a
dictionary. I don't read *any* newspaper. I am ashamed of
my incompetence. I am ashamed of how I look. Do you
know what I mean? Have you the slightest idea of what I
mean?

(*A buzzer sounds from offstage*)

BOB: Now what? (*Buzzer again*) That's him, isn't it? Down
in the lobby.

BETSY: Maybe it is.

BOB: I'm going to tell the guy to come up.

BETSY: No, Bob.

BOB: I'm going to tell the guy to come *up!* And when he
does, when he makes his so-called "declaration," I'm going to knock him DOWN!

BETSY: Bobby, no.

BOB: I am! And then I'm going to tell him to get the hell out
of our lives! (*He goes off, carrying the flowers*)

BETSY (*calling after him*): Bobby! Don't! Please! (*To audience*) He didn't hit him, thank God. Trencher never got

close enough for that. But the poor man stood in the vestibule, hat in hand, while Bob yelled and swore at him and then, when Trencher turned to go, Bob threw the vase of flowers at him, which hit him right in the small of his back.

(*Bob comes back on*)

BOB: He's gone.

BETSY: I know he's gone.

BOB: Are you crying?

BETSY: Yes.

BOB: Why?

BETSY: Why? Why am I crying? I am crying because my father died when I was twelve and my mother married a man I detested. I am crying because I had to wear an ugly dress to dancing school, and didn't have a good time. I'm crying because I'm tired and can't sleep. (*She goes upstage; looks off*)

BOB (*to audience*): Now when I come home in the evenings, Betsy and I go right to the children's room. Sometimes they have built something preposterous, and their sweetness, their compulsion to build, and the brightness of the light are reflected perfectly in Betsy's face. We feed them, we bathe them, we get them to bed. Afterwards she stands for a moment in the middle of the room, trying to make some connection between the evening and the day. Then I light the candles in the candlesticks she inherited from her grandmother . . . (*he does*) . . . and we sit down to our supper.

(Jane and Bill come on, making their way down a "row" as if for a meeting. Jane is played by Second Actress, Bill by Second Actor. We might hear an Episcopal hymn. Simultaneously the lights dim on Betsy and Bob as they carry off the lighted candles)

JANE: Excuse me . . . excuse me . . . I'm sorry . . . excuse me.

BILL: Sorry . . . are those your toes? . . . Sorry . . . excuse us, please.

(They settle into their seats. Charlie, played by First Actor, comes on and stands somewhat behind them. The Rector of St. James' School comes on to address a parents' meeting. He is played by Third Actor)

RECTOR: . . . and we believe very strongly here at St. James' that all our children should be grounded in at least one year of Latin before they go off to boarding school, and be able to play at least two team sports. Furthermore, all students are pledged to abide by the honor system. Courage, good sportsmanship and honor—these are the coin of our realm. *(Jane and Bill are now whispering animatedly between themselves)* I might conclude by pointing out that this year there are sixteen children enrolled in St. James' whose parents *and* grandparents also went here. I doubt if any other day school in the city could equal that.

JANE *(raising her hand)*: Doctor Frisbee . . .

BILL *(whispering to Jane)*: Don't.

JANE: Doctor Frisbee . . .

BILL: I warned you . . . DON'T!

JANE (*whispering to Bill*): I want to.

BILL: Goodnight, then. (*He gets up; to "others" in the row*) Excuse me . . . sorry about those toes . . . excuse me . . . goodnight . . . (*He edges his way out*)

JANE (*defiantly*): Dr. Frisbee . . .

RECTOR: Yes, Mrs. Sheridan.

JANE (*standing up*): I wonder if you have ever thought of enrolling Negro children in Saint James'?

RECTOR: Ah. (*Pause*) That question came up three years ago. A report was submitted to the board of trustees. There have been very few requests for it. (*She waits*) But if you'd like a copy, I will have one sent to you.

JANE: Yes. I would like to read it.

(*The Rector goes off. A piano now plays dancing school music, such as "Alice Blue Gown." Mrs. Bailey, the dancing school mistress, addresses the audience*)

MRS. BAILEY: We will now attempt the waltz, children. . . . One two three, one two three . . .

(*She fades off as Jane comes downstage as if to watch the class. Charlie approaches her*)

CHARLIE: Hello.

JANE: Hello.

CHARLIE: I was interested in the question you asked at the Saint James' parents meeting the other night.

JANE: I'm glad *some*one was interested. The rector wasn't. My husband certainly wasn't.

CHARLIE: That's what was interesting. (*She looks at him*) I mean, the rector's reply.

JANE: Yes . . . it just seems so dumb not to respond to the changing times.

CHARLIE: I agree.

(*They look out*)

JANE: This is dumb, too. When you think about it. Dancing school.

CHARLIE: I went. Didn't you?

JANE: Oh yes. Yes.

CHARLIE: At least it taught us to be courteous and polite.

JANE: Yes . . .

(*They watch the dancing*)

CHARLIE: Haven't we seen each other waiting for the schoolbus? At 68th and Park?

JANE: Oh yes.

CHARLIE: You have your daughter, and I have my son.

JANE (*carefully*): Somebody said your wife had died.

CHARLIE: Yes. I've remarried.

JANE: Yes.

CHARLIE (*looking out*): She's very cute, your little girl.

JANE: Not cute enough, I'm afraid. She seems to have been relegated to the sidelines.

CHARLIE: Oh well.

JANE: That velvet dress was supposed to do the trick. It was a present from my mother.

CHARLIE: I notice my boy is misbehaving again.

JANE: Mine won't even smile.

CHARLIE: I'll tell mine to dance with her next week.

JANE: If she'll come. She's becoming totally uncooperative. She's hopeless on the piano, and I drag her kicking and screaming to her riding lessons . . .

(*The music ends; they applaud*)

CHARLIE: Would you have lunch with me some time?

JANE (*immediately*): Yes.

CHARLIE: Next Tuesday? One o'clock? Rocco's, at 31st and 1st?

JANE: Sounds interesting.

CHARLIE: It's—out of the way.

JANE: That's what sounds interesting.

CHARLIE: We can talk about Saint James' School.

JANE: Yes. Oh yes.

CHARLIE (*calling out, as he crosses the stage*): Billy! Behave!

(*They are now on either side of the stage*)

JANE (*to audience*): The menu at Rocco's was soiled, and so was the waiter's tuxedo, but we met again—for dinner, when my husband was away.

CHARLIE (*to audience*): She was excited at finding someone who was interested in her opinions. Which I was. And we kissed in the taxi when I took her home.

(*They move closer to each other*)

JANE (*to audience*): And then we met in the rotunda at the Metropolitan Museum, and again for lunch at a restaurant in an uptown apartment house.

CHARLIE: The reason I asked you to come here is that my firm has an apartment upstairs.

JANE: Yes. All right.

CHARLIE: Do you want to walk up? The elevator men in these buildings . . .

JANE: I don't care about the elevator men in these buildings.

CHARLIE (*to audience*): And so we went up.

(*They step into the "elevator;" their hands touch*)

JANE (*to audience*): For lovers, touch is metamorphosis. All the parts of their bodies seem to change into something different and better.

CHARLIE: That part of their experience, the totality of years before they met, is changed and redirected toward this moment.

JANE: They feel they have reached an ecstasy of rightness that they command in every part . . .

CHARLIE: And any recollection that occurs to them takes on this final clarity . . .

JANE: Whether it be a Chicago railroad station on Christmas Eve . . .

CHARLIE: Or running a ski trail at that hour when, although the sun is still in the sky, the north face of every mountain lies in the dark.

(*They are about to kiss when Charlie's wife storms on behind them. She is played by Third Actress in raincoat and hat*)

WIFE (*pounding on the "door"*): Let me in there! Charles, I know you're in there! I can hear you! I can hear you whispering!

JANE (*whispering*): How did she . . .

CHARLIE (*whispering*): Mrs. Woodruff in the rotunda. . . . She must have told her.

WIFE (*more pounding*): All right then, Charles! I intend to call her husband immediately!

(*She storms off. Pause*)

CHARLIE: I'd better go put out the fire.

JANE: Yes. (*He goes off. Jane turns to the audience*) And then it struck her that they were all too confused to abide by the forms that guarantee the permanence of a society, as their fathers and mothers had done. (*Dancing school music again; she gets up*) Instead, they put the burden of order onto their children, and filled their days with specious rites and ceremonies . . .

(*Mrs. Bailey comes up to her. Charlie comes on in time to hear*)

MRS. BAILEY: Oh I'm so glad to see you, Mrs. Sheridan. We were afraid you were sick. Right after class began, Mr. Sheridan came and took your girl.

JANE: Took her? Where?

MRS. BAILEY: He mentioned something about Europe. He seemed very upset.

JANE: Thank you, Mrs. Bailey. (*Mrs. Bailey moves off. Charlie comes up to her*) What do we do?

CHARLIE (*whispering*): It will be all right, my darling. It will be all right.

JANE: I'm not sure it will be, at all!

(*She hurries off. He starts to follow her off*)

MRS. BAILEY (*to "class"*): Dance, children! . . . Straight backs! . . . One two three, one two three . . . (*She goes off*)

CHARLIE (*turning to audience*): I am perceived as a somewhat retiring man. Here's why . . . (*The piano waltz modulates to skating music, as if played on a Wurlitzer organ*) You may have seen my mother, waltzing on ice skates in Rockefeller Center. (*Behind him, First Actress "skates" with Third Actor*) She's seventy-eight years old, but very wiry, and she wears a red velvet costume with a short skirt. Her tights are flesh colored, and she has spectacles and a red ribbon in her hair, and she waltzes with one of the rink attendants. (*We see this*) I suppose I should be grateful for the fact that she amuses herself and is not a burden to me, but I sincerely wish she had hit on some less conspicuous recreation. Whenever I see gracious old ladies arranging chrysanthemums and pouring tea, I think of my own mother, dressed like a hatcheck girl, pushing some paid rink attendant around the ice, in the middle of the third biggest city in the world . . .

(*Harding, his father, comes out and sits in a chair at a table. Harding is played by Second Actor*)

HARDING (*calling off*): Kellner! Garçon! Cameriere! You! Could we have a little service here!

CHARLIE (*to audience*): And this was my father. My mother divorced him long ago. (*He pulls up a chair and joins Harding*) Hi, Dad.

HARDING (*still calling off*): Chop! Chop! (*To Charlie*) You hungry?

CHARLIE: Sure.

HARDING: We'll stoke you up before you have to go back to that lousy boarding school gruel. (*Calls off*) My good man! (*To Charlie*) I should have brought my whistle. I have a whistle that is audible only to the ears of old wait-

ers. (*The waiter at last arrives, played by Third Actor*)
Now, take out your little pad and your little pencil, and
see if you can get this straight: two Beefeater Gibsons.
Repeat after me: two Beefeater Gibsons.

WAITER (*an old man*): How old is the boy?

HARDING: That, my good man, is none of your goddam business.

WAITER: I'm sorry, sir, but I cannot serve the boy.

HARDING: Well, I have some news for you. I have some very
interesting news. This doesn't happen to be the only restaurant in New York. They've opened another on the corner. (*The waiter goes off*) Come on, Charlie.

(*They exchange seats as the waiter rips off the white tablecloth revealing an English print underneath*)

CHARLIE (*to audience*): And we went to an English pub . . .

HARDING (*calling off*): Heigh ho! Master of the hounds! Tallyhoo, and all that! We'd like something in the way of a
stirrup cup! (*To waiter, still played by Third Actor*) Let's
see what England can produce in the way of a cocktail!

WAITER (*Irish accent*): This isn't England.

HARDING: If there is one thing I can't tolerate, it's an impudent domestic. Come on, Charlie.

(*They exchange seats again, as the waiter reveals a redcheckered tablecloth*)

CHARLIE (*to audience*): The fifth place we went was Italian.

HARDING: *Buon giorno. Per favore, possiamo avere due cocktail americani, forti, forti. Molto gin, poco vermut.*

WAITER (*young; gay*): I don't understand Italian.

HARDING: Oh come off it! *Subito, subito.*

WAITER: I'm sorry, sir, this table is reserved.

HARDING: All right. Get us another table.

WAITER: All the tables are reserved.

HARDING: I get it. *Capeesh.* Well, the hell with you. *Vada all'inferno.* Onwards and upwards, Charlie.

(*The waiter goes off with the tablecloths. Charlie and Harding come downstage; street noises*)

CHARLIE: I've got to make my train, Dad.

HARDING: Now?

CHARLIE: I do.

HARDING: I should have taken you to my club. The service there is excellent. But for some reason, I'm no longer a member . . . Well, come on. I'll walk you to Grand Central.

CHARLIE: That's O.K., Dad.

HARDING: No, I want to. And I want to buy you a paper. A gentleman should have something to read on the train. (*A newsman comes on with newspapers, once again played by Third Actor*) Kind sir, would you be good enough to favor me with one of your goddam, no-good, ten-cent afternoon papers? (*The newsman turns away*) Is it asking too much, kind sir, for you to sell me one of your disgusting specimens of yellow journalism? (*The newsman goes*)

CHARLIE: I'm late, Dad.

HARDING: Now, just wait a second, sonny. Just wait right there. I want to get a rise out of this chap. (*He goes off, calling after the newsman*) Oh sir! Scribe! Pawn of the Fifth Estate! (*He is off*)

CHARLIE (*calling after him*): Goodbye, Daddy . . . goodbye. (*To audience*) And that was the last time I saw my father.

(*He goes off, as we hear party music, now from the Fifties. Lively and reassuring, such as Bing Crosby singing "Dear Folks and Gentle People." Others come out, enjoying the party. Everyone has drinks. Behind, the background changes to a pleasant green, as seen through a picture window. Gee-Gee comes on, slightly drunk. He is played by Third Actor. Peaches, played by First Actress, approaches him*)

PEACHES: Are you all right?

GEE-GEE (*unconvincingly*): Fine.

PEACHES (*to audience*): My husband and I have recently moved to one of the hill towns. I don't mean the real hill towns—Assisi or Perugia, perched on those three-thousand foot crags—no, I mean the towns perched north of New York.

GEE-GEE (*to audience; sardonically*): They resemble the hill towns only in that the ailing, the disheartened and the poor cannot ascend the steep moral paths that form their natural defenses.

PEACHES (*to audience*): Here life is comfortable and tranquil, and in nearly every house, there is love, graciousness and high hopes. Here the schools are excellent, the roads are smooth and—

(*Archie, played by Second Actor, comes down to them*)

ARCHIE: Welcome, welcome.

GEE-GEE: Thank you, thank you.

ARCHIE: I'm interested in your names. (*To Peaches*) Why do they call you Peaches?

PEACHES: Oh it's just a nickname. When I was little, I thought life was peaches and cream.

ARCHIE: I see. (*To Gee-Gee*) And is it true that people call you Gee-Gee?

GEE-GEE: It is.

ARCHIE: Why?

GEE-GEE: I need another drink. (*He goes to the bar*)

PEACHES (*quickly*): It's from college. At college they called him Greek God. See? G. G. He was All-America twice.

ARCHIE: What college?

PEACHES: Wisconsin. But he went to Andover before that. He was vice president of his class, and captain of the hockey team.

(*Gee-Gee returns with a drink*)

ARCHIE: Say, Gee-Gee, did you know Chucky Ewing at Andover? He must have been there when you were. He
went on to Yale, and now works for Brown Brothers Har-
riman. He married Bunny Bean from Vassar and moved
to Mamaroneck two years ago. They spend their summers
in their family's house on Fisher's Island, and . . . (*He
runs out of steam*)

GEE-GEE (*looking at him vaguely*): What?

ARCHIE: I said did you know Chucky—

GEE-GEE: God, it's stuffy in here. (*He takes off his tie*)

PEACHES (*whispering*): Oh sweetie. No.

GEE-GEE: Terribly stuffy. (*He kicks off his shoes*)

PEACHES: Gee-Gee. Please. Not our first night here.

GEE-GEE (*taking off his shirt*): I have to teach them, honey.
They've got to learn.

PEACHES (*to Archie*): He's had a little too much to drink.

GEE-GEE: Like hell I have. I haven't had half enough. (*He
chug-a-lugs his drink; shouts*) I'VE GOT TO TEACH
THEM!

(*Martha, Archie's wife, comes down to join them. She is
played by Third Actress*)

MARTHA: What do you want to teach us, Gee-Gee?

GEE-GEE (*embracing her*): You'll never know. You're all too
god-damned stuffy.

ARCHIE: You're not teaching anybody anything, Gee-Gee, but the fact that you're rotten drunk.

GEE-GEE: What a god-damned bunch of stuffed shirts! Let's put a little vitality into the conversation, shall we?

(*He starts a striptease, singing " 'Take it off, Take it off,' cried the boys from the rear . . ."*)

PEACHES (*to Martha; hoplelessly*): Oh dear. He did this in Scarsdale. He did it in Chappaqua.

MARTHA: But why?

PEACHES: I don't know. And he used to be so wonderful. (*Calls to Gee-Gee*) Come back, Gee-Gee! Come back to me! Come back to the way you were!

(*Gee-Gee is down to his boxer shorts*)

ARCHIE (*going up to him*): Get out of my house, Gee-Gee.

GEE-GEE: The pleasure's all mine, neighbor.

(*He gives Archie a big kiss, then moons the room before he exits drunkenly. A long moment*)

GUEST (*played by First Actor; to Archie, handing back his drink*): Thanks for a lovely evening.

(*He exits hurriedly with his wife, played by Second Actress*)

PEACHES (*calling after him*): Gee-Gee! Oh please! (*To the others, as she picks up his clothes*) He doesn't hear me anymore. He doesn't hear the children.

MARTHA (*helping her pick up*): I'm sorry, Peaches.

PEACHES: I know you are. But you won't be around to say
goodbye. Even the garbageman will be glad to see us go!
. . . Oh come back, Gee-Gee! Come back to me!

(*She hurries off, carrying his clothes. Pause*)

ARCHIE: I wonder what he wanted to teach us?

MARTHA (*tentatively*): I think . . . he wants to prepare us
for something.

ARCHIE: Prepare us for what?

MARTHA: I don't know . . . age. Sickness. Death.

ARCHIE: Jesus, Martha.

MARTHA: I mean, he seems to think we're all so rich and
happy . . . maybe he just wants to prepare us.

ARCHIE: Well, I wish he could prepare us without taking off
his clothes.

MARTHA: I wish he could, too. (*Archie goes off. Martha turns
to audience*) I don't know. Recently I've had this terrible
feeling that I'm a character in a television situation com-
edy. I mean, I'm nice-looking, I'm well-dressed, I have
humorous and attractive children, but I have this terrible
feeling that I'm in black-and-white and can be turned off
by anybody. I just have this terrible feeling I can be
turned *off.*

(*She goes off, as we hear mysterious music. Ethan comes
downstage with a book. He is played by First Actor. He
settles into a chair to read*)

ETHAN (*to audience*): It's late at night. I'm reading *Anna Karenina*. My wife Rachel is up in Seal Harbor with the kids, while I've stayed down here to work. Our living room is comfortable, the book is interesting and the neighborhood is quiet, what with so many people away. (*He reads, then puts down his book*) Oh hell, I might as well admit it. Rachel's left me. She's left me twice before, but this is it. Hey, that's O.K.! You can cure yourself of a romantic, carnal and disastrous marriage. But like any addict in the throes of a cure, you have to be careful of every step you take. (*The telephone rings*) Like not answering the telephone. (*Indicating the phone*) Because that's Rachel. Maybe she's repented, or wants to tell me it's rained for five days, or one of the children has a passing fever—something . . . (*Shouting at phone*) But I will not be tempted to resume a relationship that has been so miserable! (*The phone stops; he resumes reading. Cricket sounds. Then a dog barks*) That's the Barstow's dog. He barks endlessly. (*The barking stops*) That's funny. Why did he stop? (*He listens. A shadowy figure, in raincoat and hat, enters stealthily upstage. He is played by Third Actor*) Then I hear very close outside, a footstep and a cough. (*The figure coughs*) I feel my flesh get hard—you know that feeling—and know I am being watched from the picture window. (*He jumps up. The figure goes*) I flip on the outside carriage light and look out. But now the lawn is empty. (*Returns to his chair*) The next night, I leave the outside light on, settle in with my book and hear the dog bark once again. (*Barking; The figure appears downstage*) And there he is again! Now in the window above the piano . . . (*He yells*) Hey, you! Get the hell out of here! (*He grabs the phone, dials "O." The figure disappears*) Rachel is gone! There's nothing to see! . . . Oh excuse me, operator. Give me the police. (*Toward off*) Leave me alone! . . . Police? Ah, is that you, Stanley? Stanley, I want to report a prowler! . . . What? (*To audience*) He seems to think I am trying to undermine real estate val-

ues. (*To phone*) Yes. . . . All right. Goodnight, Stanley.
(*To audience*) He said he was underpaid and overworked,
and that if I wanted a guard around my house, I should
vote to enlarge the police force. (*Lights change to day-
light. We hear a train announcement: "The eight-eighteen
for Grand Central is arriving on track two." Ethan puts on
his jacket, adjusts his tie and grabs his briefcase. Herb
Marston, played by Third Actor, comes on down right, as
if onto the station platform. He wears a hat and also carries a briefcase. He looks up the track, waiting for the
train to arrive. Ethan steps onto the "platform" down left;
to audience*) The next day I see my man. He is waiting on
the platform for the eight-eighteen. It's Herb Marston,
who lives in the big yellow house on Glenhollow Road.
(*Ethan goes up to him*) Hey! I don't mind you looking in
my windows, Mr. Marston, but I wish you wouldn't tram-
ple on my wife's begonias! (*Marston checks his watch as
Ethan turns to audience*) That's what I *planned* to say. But
I didn't. Because just as I was about to let fly—

(*Herb's daughter comes on with* The New York Times. *She is
played by Third Actress*)

DAUGHTER: Here's your *Times*, Daddy.

(*His wife comes on, carrying coffee in a paper bag. She is
played by Second Actress*)

ESTHER: And coffee, for the train.

HERB: Thank you both.

(*They embrace, and go off*)

ETHAN (*to audience*): So I couldn't. How could I? With his
    wife, and that sweet daughter, right there. . . . And no-
    tice there was nothing irregular in his manner. He looked

solvent, and rested, and moral—much more so than Chucky Ewing, down the platform, who is job hunting, or —(*looks off*) uh oh. There's Grace Harris, otherwise known as Black Widow, probably off to another funeral . . . (*Grace approaches him, wearing a black coat and hat. She is played by First Actress*) Hey, why is she giving me that sad, sad look?

GRACE: You poor, poor boy.

ETHAN: I'm not poor and I'm not a boy, Grace.

GRACE: I see the noose around your neck.

(*She turns and goes off, funereally*)

ETHAN (*to audience*): The noose! How did she know about the noose? Last night I dreamed about a hangman's noose. All night long, every time I closed my eyes, there it was swinging in front of me. Does she think I plan to hang myself? Is that why Marston stands in our flower garden, waiting for me to do it? O.K. Fine. Then I'll burn every rope in the house. (*The telephone rings again; he ignores it*) And I'll stick to my cure! (*He takes up "Anna Karenina," puts his finger on an arbitrary passage, reads*) "And Anna saw that her only choice was to leap in front of the oncoming train." (*He groans, sits on the couch, but now is uncomfortable. He reaches under the cushion and pulls out an old whiffle ball*) What's this? . . . Oh my God, the kids' old whiffle ball . . . the games on the lawn . . . the sledding in winter . . . the bike trip . . . oh my God! (*He kisses the whiffle ball reverently, then the telephone rings once more. He answers quickly*) Yes! Oh my darling! (*To audience*) It's been raining up there for a week. (*To phone*) I'll drive all night! I'll be there tomorrow! Oh my love! (*To audience as he hurriedly puts on his jacket*) And after that, so far as I know, Herb

Marston no longer stands outside our house in the dark, though I see him often at the country club dances. (*He comes downstage. Street sounds*) His daughter is to be married next month, and his wife has been cited by the United Fund for—

(*Patsy comes on, played by Third Actress. She carries a paper bag*)

PATSY: Yoo hoo! Ethan!

ETHAN (*crossing to her*): Oh hello, Patsy.

PATSY: Could I ask you a rather peculiar question?

ETHAN: Shoot.

PATSY: What do Republicans drink? I mean, generally.

ETHAN: Republicans? Scotch, probably.

PATSY (*patting her bag*): That's what I thought. Scotch.

ETHAN: What does Ed say?

PATSY: Ed's away . . . thank you, Ethan. (*Ethan starts off*) Oh. And how was your summer?

ETHAN: Fine. Everything was fine. Everyone is well and happy.

(*He goes off tossing the whiffle ball. Patsy takes the Scotch out of the bag, sets it up at her bar. Door chimes*)

PATSY (*calling off*): It's open!

FRED'S VOICE (*played by Second Actor*): Hello?

PATSY (*calling off*): I'm in here.

(*She drapes herself attractively somewhere. Fred comes on*)

FRED: Good evening.

PATSY: Hello again . . . how about a drink?

FRED: A little Scotch maybe.

PATSY: Scotch? I believe I can produce Scotch. (*Goes to bar*) Yes indeedy. Scotch.

FRED: What train does your husband come in on?

PATSY (*mixing him a drink*): Him? Oh he's away. His business takes him all over the world.

FRED: What does he do?

PATSY: Him? Oh he manufactures plastic tongue depressors. They take him all over the world. (*She hands him a drink*) You know, when you called, when you said you were stopping by, I was secretly hoping you might wear your uniform.

FRED: What uniform?

PATSY: Your general's uniform.

FRED: Oh I'm not a general.

PATSY: I heard someone call you "General" after church.

FRED: Oh that. That started in the locker room at the Golf Club. I happen to have political opinions. And I happen to express those opinions.

PATSY: You mean you know things that generals know?

FRED: I believe I do. For example, I know it's time to hang tough. If the Russians want trouble, I say throw a little nuclear hardware at 'em. Show 'em who's boss. I have the courage to say these things. So Chucky Ewing started calling me "General." Never mind. Somebody has to keep watch around here.

PATSY: I couldn't agree more. (*She sits on the couch*) I'm sorry your wife is sick.

FRED: Not sick. Just tired. From her volunteer work. She does a lot of collecting. It runs in her family. Her grandmother did smallpox. Her mother does mental health. My wife is T.B. I told her I'd finish up her list. (*Sits next to her*)

PATSY: So you called me.

FRED: So I called you.

PATSY: I'd better start looking for my checkbook.

FRED (*reaching for her*): Not yet.

PATSY (*skittering away*): Hey. At ease, General . . .

FRED: I can't be gone too long.

PATSY: I want my favor first.

FRED: What favor?

PATSY: Guess.

FRED: I can't give you money. I'm not rich, you know.

PATSY: Oh I wouldn't think of taking money.

FRED: Then what is it?

PATSY: Something you wear.

FRED: My dad's watch? My Sunday cuff links?

PATSY: Something else.

FRED: Ah hah! My Zippo lighter from the war! Zippo?

PATSY: No . . . I won't tell you unless you promise to give it to me.

FRED: I never promise unless I can keep that promise.

PATSY: It's very small.

FRED: How small?

PATSY: Tiny. Weeny.

FRED (*seizing her in his arms*): Please.

PATSY: I want a key to your bomb shelter.

FRED: Who told you about that?

PATSY: I saw it with my own eyes. I saw those bulldozers and trucks. I saw you plant grass seed over it. I saw your wife put that birdbath on top of it.

FRED: Is that the reason you came up to me after church?

PATSY (*marching her fingers up and down his rib cage*): Creepy, creepy, creepy mouse . . .

FRED: That shelter was designed strictly for my family . . .

PATSY: Come to live in the general's house . . .

FRED: We've made some very tough decisions with that shelter. We've had to cut out cousins. We've had to let my Aunt Ida stay outside and burn . . .

PATSY (*seductively*): . . . the rocket's red glare . . . the bombs bursting in air . . .

FRED: All right! (*He takes a small key on a chain from around his neck*) If we hit them before they hit us, you might never have to use this.

(*She takes it, drops it down the front of her dress*)

PATSY: Thank you, General. Now for my checkbook. Suppose we take a little look upstairs . . .

(*They go off, as the lights change to dappled outdoor green. Maynard wheels on an outdoor grill. He is played by Third Actor. His wife Zena, played by Second Actress, glowers at him from a table*)

MAYNARD (*to audience*): What a splendid summer night! The light hits you like a blow. The air smells as if hundreds of wonderful girls had just wandered across the lawn. (*Cleaning the grill*) In the summer I cook most of our dinners on a charcoal grill in the backyard. Tonight we had hamburgers, and I noticed my wife Zena didn't seem to have any appetite. The children ate heartily, of course, but perhaps they sensed a quarrel, because as soon as they were through, they slipped into the television room —to watch the quarrels there.

(*He goes to clear the table*)

ZENA: You're so inconsiderate. You never think of me.

MAYNARD: I'm sorry, darling. Wasn't the hamburger done?

ZENA: It wasn't the hamburger—I'm used to the garbage you cook. It's just that your whole attitude is so inconsiderate.

MAYNARD: What have I done, darling?

ZENA: What have you done? What have you done? You've ruined my life, that's what you've done!

MAYNARD: I don't see how I've ruined your life. I guess you're disappointed—lots of people are . . . (*They both glance at the audience*) . . . but I don't think it's fair to blame it all on your marriage.

ZENA: Oh God.

MAYNARD: There are lots of things I wanted to do—I wanted to climb the Matterhorn—but I wouldn't blame the fact that I haven't on anyone else.

ZENA (*laughing*): You? Climb the Matterhorn? Ha. You couldn't even climb the Washington Monument.

MAYNARD: Sweetheart—

ZENA: You have ruined my life.

(*She goes off with the plates as Jack comes on. He carries a cooking fork and wears an apron reading "Danger! Men Cooking!" Jack is played by Second Actor*)

JACK (*to audience*): As soon as I check into the hotel in Minneapolis, the telephone's ringing. She tells me the hot-water heater isn't working. So I say why doesn't she call the plumber, and she cries. She cries over long distance for about fifteen minutes. Now there's a very good jewelry store in Minneapolis, so I bought her a pair of earrings. Sapphires. Eight hundred dollars. I give them to her when I get home. We go over to the Barnstable's for dinner, and later she tells me she's lost one. She doesn't know where. She won't even call the Barnstables to see if it's lying around on the floor. So then I say it's like throwing money into the fire, and she cries again. She says sapphires are cold stones—they express my inner coldness. She says there wasn't any love in those earrings—all I had to do was step into a jewelry store and buy them. So then I ask her does she expect me to *make* her jewelry—does she want me to go to night school and learn how to make one of those crummy silver bracelets? Hammered? You know. Every little hammer blow a sign of love and affection. Is that what she wants, for Chrissake? And that's another night I slept in the guest room . . .

(*He goes off as Maynard comes on. He wheels the grill off-stage*)

MAYNARD (*to audience*): Now it's fall, and the children have gone away to school. (*Furtively, as Zena comes on with two plates*) I think Zena is trying to poison me.

ZENA: Sit down and eat. We can at least try to watch "I've Got a Secret."

(*She turns on the "television." They sit side by side on the couch; he takes his plate*)

MAYNARD: What's this?

ZENA: What does it look like? Ham, salad and potatoes.

(*Maynard takes a bite, spits it out*)

MAYNARD: There's something wrong with the salad. (*He wipes out his mouth with his napkin*)

ZENA: Ah yes. I was afraid that would happen. You left your lighter fluid in the pantry, and I mistook it for vinegar. (*She takes his plate, and gets up*)

MAYNARD: Where are you going?

ZENA: I thought I might *try* to take a bath.

MAYNARD: Why *try*, dear? Why not just do it?

ZENA: I'll try to ignore that. (*She goes off*)

MAYNARD (*to audience*): Oh God, it could be just my imagination. Lord knows she irritates me these days. Even her manner of speaking offends me . . . "I must *try* to arrange the flowers." (*À la Dracula*) "I must *try* to buy a hat." Is it me? Am I crazy? Or has the world gone mad?

(*Maynard goes off as Burt, played by First Actor comes out in a black sweater, dark gloves and a cap. He is examining a wallet*)

BURT (*to audience*): A few weeks ago, I lost my job. I'm broke, and the bills are piling up, so tonight, after the Warburton's party, I sneaked back into their house, climbed the stairs, patted their cocker spaniel, entered their bedroom and stole Bill Warburton's wallet out of his pants. (*Opens the wallet, counts the money*) Nine hundred dollars! . . . But oh, I'm miserable! I never knew that the mind could open up so many chambers of such self-reproach! Where is my innocence? Where are the trout streams of my youth? Where is the wet-leather smell of the loud waters and the keen woods after a smashing rain? (*Puts the money back in the wallet*) At least this will pay the bills. (*He goes off, as Maynard comes back on*)

MAYNARD (*quickly*): Back to the poison. Two nights ago I came home, looked into the kitchen, and thought I saw . . . (*Zena comes on, carrying a can of pesticide*) Oh!

ZENA: Oh. It's you.

MAYNARD: What were you doing?

ZENA: What does it look like I was doing?

MAYNARD: It looked like you were putting pesticide on the lamb chops.

ZENA: I know you don't grant me much intelligence, but I think I know better than that.

MAYNARD: But then what are you doing with the pesticide?

ZENA: I was *trying* to dust the roses! (*She goes off*)

MAYNARD (*to audience*): I ate one of the lamb chops at dinner. I had to. It's a question of trust. I mean, we've been married for twenty years. Surely I know her well enough to think that she wouldn't . . . (*He belches*) That night I spent an hour in the bathroom with acute indigestion. She seemed to be asleep when I came back to bed, but I did notice her eyes were open wide! (*He glances off, hissing like a vampire*) So tonight I intend to watch. I will hide in the broom closet. (*He steps into the "closet," crouches down*) Through the keyhole I can see most of the kitchen, and observe her prepare the meal . . . (*Zena comes in, gets a drink, exits singing "Whistle While You Work"*) We always keep the pesticide on the cellar stairs . . . sure enough! There she is, taking it out! (*She goes off; he watches*) O.K., she's stepping into the garden. She must be dusting the roses . . . but now she is coming back in . . . AND SHE DID NOT RETURN THE PESTICIDE TO ITS RIGHTFUL LOCATION! It is still with her! . . . Now she is taking the meat out of the oven. She is spicing it . . . her back is to me . . . I can't quite see. . . . Is that salt and pepper she is sprinkling on the meat loaf, or is it nerve poison? . . . She's spooning out the vegetables, she's serving the meat. . . . (*He steps out of the "closet"*) And here she comes with the evening meal. (*Zena comes in, carrying the meat loaf*) Hiya.

ZENA: I think we should *try* to eat. (*She puts the meat loaf on the table in front of him*)

MAYNARD (*shoving the meat loaf toward her*): It's hot tonight, isn't it?

ZENA (*shoving it back*): You think it's hot?

MAYNARD (*sliding it to her again*): I do. Yes.

ZENA: Well. We can't expect to be comfortable, can we, if we go around hiding in broom closets! (*She shoots it into his lap*)

MAYNARD (*to audience*): And somehow we got through another meal . . .

(*Sound of thunder. They remain frozen at the table. Christina, played by First Actress, comes on in curlers, wearing a bathrobe. She carries a little notebook*)

CHRISTINA (*to audience*): Lately my husband and I have had trouble getting to sleep. Burt is temporarily unemployed,

so he relaxes by taking long walks around the neighborhood. As for me? Why, I simply review what I've done
during the course of the day. This morning, for example,
I drove Burt to the early train so he could look for another job. Then I . . . (*consults her notebook*) had the
skis repaired. Booked a tennis court. Bought the wine
and groceries because tonight was our turn to give the
monthly dinner of the *Société Gastronomique du Westchester Nord.* Attended a League of Women Voters meeting on sewers. Went to a full-dress lunch for Bobsie Neil's
aunt. Weeded the garden. Ironed a uniform for the part-
time maid who helped with the dinner. Typed two-
and-a-half pages of my paper for the book club on the
early novels of Henry James. Emptied the wastebaskets.
Helped the sitter prepare the children's supper. Gave
Ronny some batting practice. Put Lizzie's hair in pin
curls. Got the cook. Met Burt at the five-thirty-five. Took
a bath. Dressed. Greeted our guests in French at half-past
seven. Said *bon soir* to all at eleven. And that's about it.
(*Puts her notebook away*) Some people might say I am
prideful for accomplishing all this. I don't think so. All I
really am is a woman enjoying herself in a country that is
prosperous and still young. (*Burt comes on, again in dark
clothes*) Coming to bed, darling?

BURT: I think I'll take a little walk.

CHRISTINA (*kissing him*): Goodnight then, sweetheart. I have
a big day tomorrow. (*She goes off. Burt puts on his cap,
pulls on his black gloves*)

BURT (*to audience*): Tonight I have to rob again. This time, it
will be the Maitlands, Maynard and Zena, over on Hob-
byhorse Lane. They fight a lot, and then they drink a lot,
so they should sleep very soundly.

(*More thunder*)

ZENA: Sounds like rain.

MAYNARD: Would you like to talk about the weather, darling?

ZENA: No thank you.

(*They sit*)

BURT (*to audience*): Oh God! I keep thinking about my beginnings—how I was made by a riggish couple in a midtown hotel after a six-course dinner with wine. My mother told me time after time that if she hadn't had so many Old-Fashioneds beforehand, I'd still be unborn on a star.

(*Thunder. Zena gets up*)

ZENA: Now I will try to do the dishes. (*She clears the table*)

MAYNARD: I will try to help you, dear . . . (*He goes to the bar*) Say, how about a glass of port?

ZENA: You plan to drink? After dinner?

MAYNARD (*taking a bottle of port*): Want to join me?

ZENA: Well, I'll try. (*Maynard picks up the pesticide*) What do you plan to do with *that*?

MAYNARD (*ambiguously*): I thought I'd *try* to put it back. (*He goes off; she goes after him, worried, carrying the meat loaf and plates. Thunder*)

BURT (*to audience*): I doubt if they can hear the thunder now their lights are out. . . . (*The sudden sound of rain*) But then suddenly I changed my mind. I wish I could say a kindly lion set me straight. Or the strains of distant music from a church. But it was no more than the rain! The rain on my head! The smell of it flying up to my nose! Goddammit, there are ways out of my trouble. I'm not trapped. It's no skin off my elbow how I have been given the gifts of life so long as I possess them, and I possess them now: the tie between the wet grass roots and the hair that grows out of my body, the thrill of my mortality that I know on summer nights, loving my children and looking down the front of my wife's dress. I'll return what I stole as soon as I can. And now I'll go home to bed.

(*A patrolman comes on with a flashlight; he is played by Second Actor*)

PATROLMAN: Mr. Hake! What are you doing out?

BURT: Just walking the dog, Stanley. (*To audience*) Even though I didn't own one. (*He calls off*) Here, Toby! Here, Toby!

STANLEY: Goodnight, Mr. Hake. Sweet dreams.

BURT: You too, Stanley. (*He goes off calling and whistling*) Good boy! Good dog! (*Stanley looks after him as the lights fade to black. End of Act One.*)

Act Two _____

BEFORE THE CURTAIN: summery music.

AT RISE: A summer seashore light. The sound of waves and gulls. Virginia, played by First Actress, comes out and takes a dust cover off a couch. She folds it as she speaks.

VIRGINIA (*to audience*): Each year we rent a house in the mountains or at the edge of the sea. I have never known the people we have rented from, but their ability to leave behind them a sense of physical and emotional presence is amazing. Someone was enormously happy here, and we rent their happiness as we rent their beach or their canoe. (*Paul comes on, in shirtsleeves, carrying his jacket, hat and briefcase. He is tying his necktie. He is played by Third Actor*) Who, we wonder, is the lady in the portrait in the upstairs hallway? Whose was the Aqualung, the set of Virginia Woolf? Who hid the copy of *Fanny Hill* in the china closet? And who painted red enamel on the toenails of the claw-footed bathtub? (*She goes off as Paul comes downstage*)

PAUL (*calling off*): Mr. Kaziac! . . . Mr. Kaziac! Would you come up to the house a minute, please! (*To the audience, as he ties his tie*) There is a moment on Sunday when the tide of a summer day turns inexorably toward the evening train back to the city. You can swim, play tennis or take a nap, but it doesn't make much difference. You are faced with the same apprehensiveness you felt in the Army as a furlough came to an end . . . (*Kaziac comes on, in coveralls, carrying a shovel. He is played by Second Actor*) Ah. Mr. Kaziac. I wonder if I might speak to you a moment before I catch my train back to the city. (*He gestures for him to sit*)

KAZIAC (*Polish accent*): Yes sir?

PAUL (*after insisting Kaziac sit*): Last Friday night, on the way from the station, I stopped to buy some rabbits for my children. I thought they might enjoy having some summer pets, particularly since I can't be with them during the week.

KAZIAC: Yes sir.

PAUL: I put those rabbits down in that old chicken house. You may have noticed them when you were down there, cutting the grass.

KAZIAC: Yes sir.

PAUL: Now it is Sunday, Mr. Kaziac, and those rabbits are dead. The children went down this morning to play with them, and found them all dead. You may imagine their shock and disappointment.

KAZIAC (*getting up*): I'll bury them, sir.

PAUL: I already have, Mr. Kaziac. I've buried them in the garden.

KAZIAC: The skunks will dig 'em up. You should of let me deal with them.

PAUL: You're a Communist, aren't you, Mr. Kaziac?

KAZIAC: No sir.

PAUL: Yes you are. You were a Communist in Poland, and you're a Communist here.

KAZIAC: Not a Communist, sir.

PAUL: I saw that newspaper you were reading. "Luxury Living Weakens U.S." Do you think luxury living has weakened me?

KAZIAC: Sir?

PAUL: Do you think you'll bury us, Mr. Kaziac? Just the way I buried those rabbits?

KAZIAC (*starting off*): I go now.

PAUL: Mr. Kaziac. Those rabbits were poisoned. I found poison in the chicken house.

KAZIAC: Yes?

PAUL: Did you put that poison there, Mr. Kaziac?

KAZIAC: No.

PAUL (*coming close to him*): Mr. Kaziac! I am serious! Don't you know how strong that poison is? Don't you know the children might have gotten into it? Don't you know it might have killed *them?* Did you do it? Did you? Oh Kaziac, listen: I have to work in the city Monday through Friday, but if you touch my children, if you harm them in any way—IN ANY WAY—I swear I'll take that shovel and cut your head open!

(*He indicates Kaziac is to leave. Kaziac looks at him, then goes off. Virginia comes back on, carrying his suitcase*)

VIRGINIA: What was that all about?

PAUL: Never mind. Just establishing a firm understanding around here.

VIRGINIA (*helping him with his jacket*): Well. Say goodbye to the children, and I'll bring the car around. (*She starts out, then stops*) Oh. I found yet another list from the owners. They say don't go near the old chicken house. They put rat poison in it last fall. That must have killed those poor bunnies. (*She goes off*)

(*A long moment. Then Paul puts on his hat, takes his suitcase*)

PAUL (*to audience; brightly*): No harm done.

(*Sound of train pulling in; Paul steps on to a "railway platform." A conductor comes on, played by First Actor. He places a step near the exit*)

CONDUCTOR: All aboard!

PAUL: No harm.

CONDUCTOR: Sir? Were you speaking to me?

PAUL (*brightly, as he climbs aboard the "train"*): No harm at all.

(*The conductor follows after, hoisting up the step as Wally, a young college boy, backs onto the stage with a football, as if to throw a long pass. He wears a sweatshirt and cutoffs, and is played by Second Actor. Sounds of surf and gulls. Bright beach light*)

WALLY (*shouting off, to receiver*): Off! Off! Way off!

(*He is about to throw the pass. Claire comes on imperiously, played by Third Actress*)

CLAIRE: You there! Young man! (*He holds his pass, looks at her*) Aren't you an Osgood?

WALLY: Excuse me?

CLAIRE (*scrutinizing him*): You *are* an Osgood, aren't you? Let me see . . . you must be out of Sally Scott by Jack Osgood, Junior.

WALLY: Actually I am.

CLAIRE: Of course you are. I recognized the nose . . . well. Go, go. Play ball. (*Wally looks at her, then goes off, perplexed, rubbing his nose. Claire turns to the audience*) In the summer months, the northeastern coast seems to be transformed into a vast social clearinghouse. If you sit on the veranda at the beach club, listening to the heavy furniture of the North Atlantic, figures from your social past appear in the surf, thick as raisins in a cake. A wave takes form, boils and breaks, revealing Consuelo Roosevelt and Mr. and Mrs. Dundas Vanderbilt, with the children of both marriages. Then a roller comes in from the right like a cavalry charge, bearing, on a rubber raft, Emerson Crane's second wife and the Bishop of Pittsburgh in an inner tube. Soon a wave breaks at your feet with the noise of a slammed trunk lid, and—

(*Her daughter Carol comes on, carrying a tennis racquet, played by First Actress*)

CAROL: Mother! The Whitneys want you to join them for lunch! They asked me, but I hate just tagging along. Maybe I'll bike into town.

CLAIRE (*vaguely*): The ocean makes you think.

CAROL (*looking out*): I suppose it does.

CLAIRE: It brings up your past. (*Looks at her*) Now you've graduated from Farmington, I think it's time I told you that during the war I was in charge of a canteen at the Embarcadero. I gave myself to many lonely soldiers. (*She goes quickly upstage, assumes a pensive pose*)

CAROL (*stunned; to audience*): At first I thought it was a lie, but Mother had never lied. Yet if what she said was true, that means she has been a fraud. Her accent is a fraud, her tastes are fraudulent and the seraphic look she assumes when she listens to music is simply the look of someone trying to recall an old telephone number. But what can I do? My father has long since gone, and I'm too young to make a life on my own. (*Pause*) So I decided my mother had not said what she said. (*Hurrying after Claire*) Mother! Mother! I've decided to join you and Whitneys!

(*They both go off as Rob comes on, played by Second Actor. He wears a bathrobe. It is now night*)

ROB (*to audience*): Outside the window, we hear the percussive noise of the sea. It shakes the bluff where the house stands, and sends its rhythm up through the plaster and the timbers of the place. We shake up a drink, send the children to bed and make love in a strange room that smells of someone else's soap. In the middle of the night, the terrace door flies open with a crash, though there seems to be no wind. I go down to see . . .

(*Nell, his wife, comes on in a bathrobe, half-asleep. She is played by Second Actress*)

NELL (*half-asleep*): Oh why have they come back?

ROB (*putting his arm around her*): No one's come back, darling. It was just the terrace door.

NELL (*still sleepily*): Why have they come back? What have they lost?

ROB: Come on, sweetheart. Come back to bed. (*He puts his arm around her*) It was nothing.

(*He takes her off as Rick comes on, played by First Actor. He wears a bathrobe and is drying his hair with a towel. Sounds of gulls and the sea*)

RICK (*to audience*): Whenever I swim, I try to avoid my old serviceable sidestroke. I practice the overhand stroke that seems to be obligatory these days. Nowadays the sidestroke is Lower Class. I saw it once in a swimming pool, and when I asked who the swimmer was, I was told he was the butler. When the ship sinks, when the plane ditches, I will try to reach the life raft with my overhand stroke, and will at least drown stylishly, whereas if I use a Lower Class sidestroke, who knows? I might live forever.

(*Charlotte, his mother, comes out with a bowl of wildflowers which she begins to arrange. She is played by Second Actress*)

CHARLOTTE: Look what I bought along the road.

RICK: They're pretty, Mother.

CHARLOTTE: Well, I thought since I'm visiting, I should at least make some contribution to the domestic tranquility.

RICK: Thank you, Mother.

CHARLOTTE: I so love flowers. I can't live without them. Should I suffer financial reverses and have to choose between flowers and groceries, I believe I would choose flowers.

RICK: Did you have a good lunch, Mother?

CHARLOTTE: The beach club has changed from the old days. Your father and I had lunch there years ago, when we visited the Pommeroys. Now it is very much changed.

RICK: How do you mean?

CHARLOTTE: They've let down the bars.

RICK: I don't understand.

CHARLOTTE (*brightly*): They're letting in Jews.

RICK: Maybe we'd better change the subject.

CHARLOTTE: I don't see why. It's a fact of life.

RICK: My *wife* is Jewish, Mother!

CHARLOTTE: That's not the point. Her father is Italian. He bears a very distinguished Northern Italian name.

RICK: Her mother was a Polish Jew. And you know it very well.

CHARLOTTE: Well, I come from old Massachusetts stock, and I'm not ashamed of it.

RICK: Nobody's ashamed, Mother.

CHARLOTTE: You seem embarrassed of your roots. This morning I heard you say tom*ay*toe, rather than tom*ah*toe.

RICK: It's just easier.

CHARLOTTE: Anyway, I like Jews.

Jack Gilpin (*left*) with Julie Hagerty in the
1994 Playwrights Horizons production.

All photos © T. Charles Erickson

Jennifer Van Dyck (*left*) with Robert Stanton in the
1994 Playwrights Horizons production.

Robert Stanton (*left*) with Mary Beth Peil in the
1994 Playwrights Horizons production.

(*Seated from left to right*) Robert Stanton, Mary Beth Peil and John Cunninham; (*standing from left to right*) Julie Hagerty, Jennifer Van Dyck and Jack Gilpin in the 1994 Playwrights Horizons production.

RICK: Oh good, Mother. Good for you.

CHARLOTTE: They work terribly hard.

RICK: They do, they do.

CHARLOTTE: They work much harder than we do.

RICK: Some do, some don't.

CHARLOTTE: Your father said they're constantly doing business. They're up at dawn doing business, and stay at it straight through cocktails. That's why they're not terribly good at tennis.

RICK: Your logic eludes me, Mother.

CHARLOTTE: And they love the telephone. They talk on the telephone all the time. Your father knew a Jew who put a telephone in his bathroom.

RICK: Impossible.

CHARLOTTE: Now me, I hate the telephone. Always have. How can you talk to someone when you can't see them. For all I know, they could be making faces at you.

RICK: They probably are.

CHARLOTTE: I suppose the Jews don't care if people do that. They don't worry about the amenities.

RICK: Mother, stop it. We are more like the Jews than you'll ever imagine.

CHARLOTTE: How, pray tell?

RICK: Because both we and the Jews know how it feels to be exiles in our native land.

CHARLOTTE: Now *that* is probably the silliest thing you've said since I've arrived.

RICK (*with a sigh*): I think I'll take another swim.

CHARLOTTE (*taking flowers off*): Do you suppose your dear Rachel would mind if I put these flowers in the dining room? If she does, I'll try to persuade her otherwise. Tactfully, though. I promise I'll be tactful.

RICK: I'm sure you will be, Mother. (*She goes off. Rick looks after her then exits another way, muttering*) Sunday . . . she's leaving Sunday . . .

(*John comes on immediately, repairing a pulley from his boat. He wears a windbreaker and is played by Second Actor. Suddenly we hear a very loud recording of the Beatles' "Sergeant Pepper's Lonely Hearts Club Band" coming from offstage*)

JOHN (*calling off*): Turn that down, please! (*The music gets louder*) Would somebody please turn that thing DOWN!

(*The music subsides. Janet comes out. She wears a man's shirt and shorts and is played by Third Actress*)

JANET: You don't have to shout, Daddy.

JOHN: I'm afraid I do, since your friend Peter apparently has a hearing disability.

JANET: We happen to like music, Daddy. (*She goes off*)

JOHN (*calling after her*): I'm not sure that you do. You used to put four or five records on the changer back in Bedford, and then walk out of the house. I never understood why. (*She comes back on, eating something*) Once I went out to see if I could find you and, standing on the lawn, I thought I understood. You liked to hear music pouring out of the windows. You liked to come back to a house where music was playing. Was that it? Was I right?

JANET: Oh Daddy, I don't know. (*She starts off*)

JOHN: Well, now you're here, does it have to be that *loud?* Night and day, your friend Peter—

JANET (*interrupting*): You don't like him, do you, Daddy?

JOHN: I like him fine.

JANET: I can tell you don't.

JOHN: I don't know him very well.

JANET: He's very sensitive.

JOHN: I should imagine. With that hair and beard, he reminds me of some minor apostle in a third-rate Passion Play.

JANET: He's the kindest person I've ever known.

JOHN: Let's talk about you, shall we, sweetheart? We didn't ask Peter to visit us this summer, we asked you. I want to know where you intend to live.

JANET (*sprawling somewhere*): With him, Daddy. I told you.

JOHN: I understand that. But where? And on what?

JANET: We'll get a place in the East Village.

JOHN: The East Village?

JANET: We'll find something.

JOHN: Suppose I bought him off.

JANET: Bought him *off?*

JOHN: Gave him some money. Sent him abroad.

JANET: He's *been* abroad, Daddy! He spent a year in India.

JOHN: Well, perhaps he should be introduced to Western Europe.

JANET: If you sent him abroad, Daddy, you know what he'd do? He'd go right to East Berlin.

JOHN: East *Berlin?*

JANET: Yes! And he'd give his passport to some creative person so they could escape to the free world.

JOHN: Why doesn't he just paint "Peace" on his ass and jump off the Eiffel tower?

JANET (*starting out*): I won't take this, Daddy.

JOHN: Sweetheart, come back. I'm sorry. (*She stops*) I just want to know what you plan to do with your life? (*He tries to put his arm around her*)

JANET (*breaking away*): I don't know. Nobody my age knows. (*She sprawls somewhere else*)

JOHN: Lots of people know, darling. I know at least fifty
girls your age who know what they want to do. They want
to be historians, editors, doctors and mothers. They want
to do something useful.

JANET: I plan to get a job.

JOHN: What kind of a job? You're not trained for anything.

JANET: I'll get a job in some office.

JOHN: Doing what?

JANET: Filing. Something. There are jobs.

JOHN: Oh my God, oh my God! After the sailing lessons and
the skiing lessons, after the get-togethers and the cotil-
lions, after the year in Florence, and the summer out
West, you plan to end up as some filing clerk!

JANET: Daddy—

JOHN: Some filing clerk, whose principal excitement will be
to go once or twice a year to a fourth-rate Chinese restaurant with your "girlfriends" and get tipsy on two sweet
Manhattans!

JANET: That does it, Daddy! That really does it! (*She goes
off*)

JOHN (*following her*): Oh sweetheart, come home. Come
home and stay and get your feet on the ground!

(*He goes off as we hear sounds of a ferry arriving: bells and
horns. Baxter comes on, played by First Actor. He wears
seersucker trousers and a sweater slung over his shoulders*)

BAXTER (*to audience*): In the middle of the summer, for those of us who don't have to work on the mainland, the tennis courts get a little dusty, the golf courses lose their green and even the sailing breezes don't seem as fresh. So on the first Monday in August, during the changing of the guard, I like to go down to meet the ferry and check out the new arrivals, just for something to do. (*Clarissa comes on, idly. She is played by First Actress. He looks her over*) This summer seemed to produce a particularly attractive crop. (*Clarissa stands waiting for someone*) Now every woman has some key. And every man is fascinated by locks. So that's what I do in August—I become a locksmith. (*To Clarissa*) Hello there.

CLARISSA: Hello.

(*Mrs. Ryan, her mother-in-law, comes on, played by Third Actress*)

MRS. RYAN: Clarissa, I've got the car!

BAXTER (*bowing politely*): Hello, Mrs. Ryan.

MRS. RYAN: Ah Baxter. This is my new daughter-in-law, Clarissa. She's taking the house for August.

BAXTER: And where's Larry?

CLARISSA: Larry is in France. He's—

MRS. RYAN: He's gone there for the government.

CLARISSA: He won't be back till the fall. And Mother Ryan's going, too.

MRS. RYAN: I don't think you need to tell Baxter our life story, Clarissa.

BAXTER (*to Clarissa*): So you'll be here by yourself?

MRS. RYAN: No! Clarissa will have houseguests right through Labor Day.

CLARISSA: But I—

MRS. RYAN (*taking Clarissa's arm*): We should hurry, dear. I'm double parked. (*As they go off*) Be careful of that man, Clarissa. He's been divorced twice and is known as a terrible roué.

CLARISSA: What's a roué? (*They are off*)

BAXTER (*to audience*): I'd heard about her, actually. She comes from Chicago, and supposed to be as stupid as she is beautiful.

(*Square dance music: Clarissa comes on. Baxter approaches her*)

BAXTER: Don't you like to dance?

CLARISSA: I love to dance. But that's not dancing. I don't believe in skipping and hopping. That's only for maids.

BAXTER: Maybe you'd like to go home.

CLARISSA: I can't. I came with the Hortons.

BAXTER: That's no reason why you have to go home with them.

CLARISSA (*considering it*): That's very true.

BAXTER (*offering his arm*): So let me do the honors. (*He leads her to a bench which becomes a "car." He opens the "door" for her. She settles onto the "seat," as he crosses around front and gets into the "driver's seat." He starts the "car." They drive. After a moment)* What about your houseguests?

CLARISSA: What houseguests?

BAXTER: I thought you had houseguests all summer.

CLARISSA: Oh, my mother-in-law just said that to ward off the men.

BAXTER: Then you're alone.

CLARISSA: I certainly am not. Wacky's there.

BAXTER: Wacky?

CLARISSA: My dog.

BAXTER: Ah. *(They drive)* You're lovely, Clarissa.

CLARISSA: That's just my outward self. Nobody knows the real me.

BAXTER *(to audience; as he drives)*: What was the key? Did she think of herself as an actress? A Channel swimmer? An heiress?

(They drive)

CLARISSA *(looking out)*: Those stones on the point. They've grown a lot since I visited last year.

BAXTER: What?

CLARISSA: You can see, even in the moonlight. Those stones have grown.

BAXTER: Stones don't grow, Clarissa.

CLARISSA: Oh yes they do. Stones grow. There's a stone in our rose garden that's grown a foot.

BAXTER (*ironically*): I didn't know stones grew.

CLARISSA: Well, they do.

BAXTER: Ah.

(*They drive*)

BAXTER: Where'd you go to school, Clarissa?

CLARISSA: I went to Miss Hall's School in Pittsfield, Massachusetts. I hear it's now gone belly up.

BAXTER: How about college?

CLARISSA: I didn't go to college.

BAXTER: No?

CLARISSA: I don't believe in college. I think college can be a waste of time and money. I mean, if you have thoughts, you have thoughts, and college professors get paid much too much trying to confuse those thoughts.

BAXTER: Ah. (*Pulling up the "car"*) Well, here we are.

CLARISSA: Yes. Here we are.

BAXTER: May I come in?

CLARISSA: No. You don't understand the kind of woman I am. Nobody does.

BAXTER: I'd like to find out. (*He leans over and tries to kiss her. Clarissa pushes him away and gets out of the "car." She speaks through the "window"*) Now you've ruined everything. I know what you've been thinking. Most men do. Well, you needn't think it any longer. I'm going to write an airmail letter to Larry in France and tell him you tried to kiss me.

BAXTER (*quickly getting out of the "car"*): I just want to know you better, Clarissa.

CLARISSA: Oh yes. Oh sure. Everyone thinks I'm dumb. Larry never lets me speak and Mother Ryan says I'm stupid, and even my houseguests said I was kind of slow.

BAXTER: I think you're intelligent.

CLARISSA: You don't mean that.

BAXTER: I do. You have a wonderful intelligence. A wonderful mind.

CLARISSA: Nobody ever takes me seriously until they get their arms around me.

BAXTER: No, no. I imagine you have a lot of very interesting opinions.

CLARISSA: I do actually. For example, I think we're like cogs in a wheel. Do you think we're like cogs in a wheel?

BAXTER: Oh yes. Oh absolutely.

CLARISSA: Do you think women should work?

BAXTER: I'm interested in *your* opinion, Clarissa.

CLARISSA: My opinion is, I don't think married women should work. Unless they have a lot of money. So they can get a maid. But even then, I think it's a full-time job to take care of a man. I don't think that working or joining the church is going to change everything, or special diets, either. I eat what's reasonable. If ham is reasonable, I buy ham. If lamb is reasonable, I buy lamb. Don't you think that's intelligent?

BAXTER: I think that's very intelligent.

CLARISSA: But progressive education. I don't buy that. When we go to the Howards' for dinner, the children ride their bikes around the table all the time, and it's my opinion they get this way from progressive schools, and that children ought to be told what's nice and what isn't.

BAXTER: You're very intelligent, Clarissa.

CLARISSA: You really think so?

BAXTER: I do. I really do.

CLARISSA: Thank you, Baxter.

(*He tries to kiss her again. She lets him*)

BAXTER: You've got lovely hair, Clarissa.

CLARISSA: It isn't as pretty as it used to be. But I'm not going to dye it. I don't think women should dye their hair.

BAXTER: That's intelligent, too. I love your intelligence, Clarissa.

CLARISSA: Thank you very much. (*She starts to lead him off*)

BAXTER (*over his shoulder to the audience as they go*): And that was the key! It was as simple as that!

(*Chaddy comes out immediately, played by Third Actor*)

CHADDY (*to audience*): The branch of the family to which we belong was founded by a minister who was eulogized by Cotton Mather. We were ministers until the middle of the nineteenth century, and the harshness of our thought is preserved in books and sermons. Man is full of misery, they say, and all earthly beauty is lustful and corrupt.

(*Mournful sea-sounds: bell-buoys and foghorns. Lawrence comes on, carrying a wooden shingle. He is played by Second Actor*)

LAWRENCE: Look at this.

CHADDY: What?

LAWRENCE: This shingle. This shingle must be over two hundred years old.

CHADDY: And?

LAWRENCE: And? *And?* This house was built in the twenties. Grampa must have bought shingles from all the farms around here just to make it look venerable.

CHADDY: I guess he did.

LAWRENCE: I *know* he did. Look. You can still see the carpenter's chalk where this shingle was nailed into place. And if you look at the front door, which is a relatively new door, you'll see that the surface has been deeply scored, and white paint has been rubbed in to imitate rot.

CHADDY: O.K., Lawrence. O.K.

LAWRENCE: Imagine spending thousands of dollars to make a sound house look like a wreck. Imagine the frame of mind this implies. Imagine wanting to live so much in the past that you'll pay carpenter's wages to disfigure your front door.

CHADDY: Maybe we should hit a tennis ball, Lawrence. Let's hit a tennis ball.

LAWRENCE: You know why, don't you? You know why we retreat into the past.

CHADDY: No, why, Lawrence?

LAWRENCE: Because we, and our friends, and our part of the nation, can't cope with the present. That's why we have to have candles when we eat. That's why we fight over old furniture.

CHADDY: Who's fighting? We all agreed you could have the highboy, Lawrence. Since apparently it means so much to you.

LAWRENCE: Grampa left it to me. And you personally have resented it ever since.

CHADDY: Come out of it, Lawrence.

LAWRENCE: Come out of what?

CHADDY: This gloominess, buddy. Come out of it. You're spoiling your own good time and everyone else's. You've made everything tense and unpleasant all weekend. You think you know everything, but you don't, Lawrence. You don't know the half of it.

LAWRENCE: I'll tell you what I know. I know our sister is promiscuous. I know Dad is almost broke. I know Mother's an alcoholic. And . . . (*tapping him with the shingle*) I know you're a superficial fool.

CHADDY (*pushing him away*): And you're a gloomy son of a bitch!

LAWRENCE (*shoving him*): Get your fat face out of mine!

(*They wrestle. Finally Chaddy pins Lawrence underneath. Chaddy raises his fist. They freeze*)

CHADDY (*to audience*): And I think I could have killed my brother then and there.

MRS. NUDD'S VOICE (*from off*): Boys!

CHADDY (*to audience*): But then my mother came and turned the hose on us.

(*They jump up sputtering and step apart. Mrs. Nudd appears with a hose and nozzle*)

MRS. NUDD: Boys! . . . Stop it! . . . Do something useful for the rest of the day! Do something with your children! Do something! (*She goes off imperiously. Pause*)

LAWRENCE: That does it, you know. That really does it. This is my last summer here, I can tell you that! If it weren't for my kids, I'd leave right now! But after this weekend, you can count me out! And I'm taking my highboy with me!

(*He strides off angrily. Immediately the lights brighten. We hear bird songs*)

CHADDY (*to audience*): And then what do you know? Suddenly the sun came out. (*He stretches in the sun*) What a morning! Jesus, what a morning! The wind is northerly, the weather is clear and Mother's roses smell like strawberry jam! (*He looks where Lawrence has gone*) Oh what can you do with a man like that? What can you do? How can you dissuade his eye in a crowd from seeking out the cheek with acne, the infirm hand: how can you teach him to respond to the inestimable greatness of the race, the harsh surface beauty of life? (*Looks out*) The sea that morning was iridescent and dark. My wife and my sister were swimming now, and I saw their uncovered heads, black and gold in the dark water. I saw them come out and I saw that they were naked, unshy, beautiful and full of grace, and I watched the naked women walk out of the sea.

(*He closes his eyes dreamily. His sister Esther comes on in a bathrobe, drying her hair with a towel. She is played by Third Actress. She comes behind him, puts her hands over his eyes*)

ESTHER: Chaddy, don't you dare tell Mother, but you know what I did last week on my trip to New York?

CHADDY: What?

ESTHER: I auditioned for an Off-Broadway play.

CHADDY: No!

ESTHER: I did! I walked into an office where there were four men. They were very circumspect, but they said I'd have to be nude.

CHADDY: Come on!

ESTHER: It's true! I'd be expected to simulate, or perform, copulation twice during the performance, and participate in a love pile at the end that involved the audience.

CHADDY: Good God! So you walked out?

ESTHER: Not at all. They asked me to take off my clothes, and I wasn't the least embarrassed. The only thing that worried me was that my feet might get dirty.

CHADDY: Jesus, Esther!

ESTHER: There I sat, naked, before these strangers, in front of a big photograph of Ethel Barrymore.

CHADDY: I can't believe this!

ESTHER: No, listen: I felt for the first time that I'd found myself, Chaddy. I felt like a new woman, a better woman. It was one of the most exciting experiences I've ever had.

CHADDY: Have you told Bill?

ESTHER: I'll cross that bridge if I get the part.

CHADDY: I'm disgusted, Esther.

ESTHER: Oh yes? Well, that's the trouble with this family. You're all so square and stuffy. You have no idea how wonderful and rich and strange life can be when you stop playing out those roles your parents designed for you. (*She goes off*)

CHADDY (*following her*): You'll never get the part, Esther! What about your stretch marks?

(*He is off, as the light changes to evening light. Nostalgic music. Mr. Nudd comes on, makes a drink. He is played by First Actor. After a moment, Mrs. Nudd comes on, played by First Actress*)

MR. NUDD: Want a drink?

MRS. NUDD: It's a little early.

MR. NUDD: It's Labor Day.

MRS. NUDD (*immediately*): Then please!

MR. NUDD (*making gin and tonics at the "bar"*): I just made another rule.

MRS. NUDD: What?

MR. NUDD: No grandchildren or dogs may enter this room for the next hour and a half.

MRS. NUDD: That is an excellent rule. (*He brings her a drink*) Thank you, darling.

MR. NUDD (*looking off and out*): Look at that light! Oh we're at our best in this light! We are at our very best.

(*Their daughter Joan comes out warily. She is played by Second Actress. She carries a letter*)

JOAN: Are you two busy? Tell me the truth.

MR. NUDD: We're busy drinking.

MRS. NUDD: Of course we're not busy.

JOAN: I've got a proposition to make.

MR. NUDD: Uh oh.

JOAN: I've decided that I won't go back to town with you tomorrow. I've decided I'll stay here for a little while longer.

MRS. NUDD: Oh now . . .

JOAN: No, there's nothing for me to do in New York. I'm just a divorced woman rattling around. I wrote to Helen Parker asking her to stay with me, and she thinks it's a great idea. I have her letter right here. Read it. Read what she says. (*She hands Mrs. Nudd the letter*)

MR. NUDD: Joan, dear. You can't stay here in the winter.

JOAN: Oh yes I can, yes I can, Daddy. We're willing to rough it. We'll take turns walking to the village for groceries.

MRS. NUDD (*handing the letter back*): But darling. The house wasn't built to be lived in during the winter. The walls are thin. The water will be turned off.

JOAN: We don't care about water, Mummy—we'll get our water from the old ice pond.

MR. NUDD: Sweetheart, you'd last about a week. I'd have to come up and get you, and I don't want to close this house twice.

JOAN: I want to stay. I've planned it for so long!

MRS. NUDD: You're being ridiculous, Joan.

JOAN: I've never asked you for anything. You've always been so strict. You've never let me do what I want.

MR. NUDD: Be reasonable, darling. Please try and imagine . . .

JOAN (*exploding*): Esther got everything she wanted. She went to Europe twice. She had that car in college. She had that fur coat. (*She sits on the floor*) I want to stay, I want to stay, I want to stay!

MRS. NUDD: Joan, you're acting like a child.

JOAN (*on the floor*): I want to act like a child! Is there anything so terrible about wanting to act like a child for a little while? I don't have any joy in my life anymore. When I'm unhappy, I try to remember a time when I was happy, but I can't remember a time anymore.

MRS. NUDD: Joan, get up. Get up on your own two feet.

JOAN: I can't, I can't, it hurts to stand up—it hurts my legs.

MR. NUDD: Get up, Joanie. (*He stoops down, helps her up*) Oh my baby. My little girl. (*He puts his arm around her, leads her in*) Come inside, and I'll wash your face. (*He takes her in, looking over his shoulder at his wife*)

MRS. NUDD (*to audience*): What makes the summer always an island? What makes it such a small island? And why do these good and gentle people who have surrounded me all my life seem like figures in a tragedy? What mistakes have we made? We have loved our neighbors, respected the force of modesty, held honor above gain . . . where have we gone wrong?

(*Chaddy comes out, with a checkerboard*)

CHADDY: Checkers, Mother?

MRS. NUDD: Now *that's* a good idea, Chaddy. Checkers.

(*Chaddy gets himself a drink*)

CHADDY: Do I look thirty-seven, Mother?

MRS. NUDD: Stop talking about your age, Chaddy. Do you realize that's all you've done, all Labor Day. Talk about your age.

CHADDY: I haven't talked about just that, Mother. I've talked about my problems at work. I've talked about the sailing races, I've talked about the kids' lousy schools . . .

MRS. NUDD: Ssshhh. Feel that refreshing breeze.

(*Chaddy sets up the checkers on the floor in front of his mother. Esther comes on*)

ESTHER: "Feel that refreshing breeze." . . . Children drown, beautiful women are mangled in automobile accidents, cruise ships founder and men die lingering deaths in mines and submarines, but you will find none of that here. Here it boils down to "feel that refreshing breeze."

(*Mrs. Nudd laughs*)

SECOND ACTOR'S VOICE (*shouting; from off*): Anyone seen my bathing suit?

CHADDY: Hey, Esther. Who are those strange people renting next door?

MRS. NUDD: They're not strange. They're cousins of the Ewings. Which makes it all the more surprising.

SECOND ACTOR'S VOICE (*from off*): I said, have you seen my bathing trunks?

SECOND ACTRESS'S VOICE (*from off*): They're kicking around underfoot somewhere.

SECOND ACTOR'S VOICE: I'm just talking about an innocent pair of bathing trunks! You make it sound as if they had been wandering around the house, drinking whiskey and breaking wind . . .

MRS. NUDD (*with Esther conducting*): Feel that refreshing breeze. (*Mr. Nudd comes back out*) Everything all right with Joan?

MR. NUDD: It will be, it will be. . . . I'm seriously thinking of lighting a fire.

ESTHER: Oh do that, Daddy. What a good idea. (*She steps over the checkerboard*)

MRS. NUDD: Esther.

ESTHER: Oh. Excuse me, Mother.

MRS. NUDD: There's a box of candy somewhere.

ESTHER: It's stale, Mother.

MRS. NUDD: It's perfectly fine. Does anyone feel like candy?

CHADDY: Actually I think the kids ate it, Mother.

MRS. NUDD: Oh.

(*Offstage Voices are heard again*)

SECOND ACTRESS'S VOICE: You goddam fucked-up no-good piece of shit! You can't make a nickel, you don't have a friend in the world and in bed you stink!

SECOND ACTOR'S VOICE: Look who's talking about bed!

SECOND ACTRESS'S VOICE: Listen: when I come, when I really come, pictures fall off the walls!

MRS. NUDD, ESTHER, CHADDY AND MR. NUDD (*all together*): Feel that refreshing breeze.

(*Joan comes back out*)

JOAN: I apologize for my dumb idea.

MR. NUDD: That's all right, darling.

JOAN: My shrink says it's good to express your feelings. But still I must have—

MR. NUDD (*interrupting*): Joanie, Joanie, make yourself a drink.

(*She does. Lawrence comes out*)

LAWRENCE: Good Lord! You're all not drinking *already!*

MRS. NUDD: We are, Lawrence, dear. And I'll thank you not to make an issue of it.

MR. NUDD: Where's Ruth? Where's your sweet Jane, Chaddy?

ESTHER: Holding the fort.

CHADDY: Playing Capture the Flag with the kids.

MRS. NUDD: What fun.

LAWRENCE: By the way, I'm taking the highboy, Mother. I plan to strap it on my station wagon.

MRS. NUDD: So we have heard, dear. Since the weekend began.

ESTHER: Remember the day the pig fell in the well?

MRS. NUDD: That was your tennis summer, wasn't it, Esther? That was the summer you played tennis with Russell.

LAWRENCE: That wasn't *all* she played with Russell that summer.

ESTHER: Dry up, Lawrence! I mean it! . . . (*She looks out*) When I get back to New York, I plan to go to work somewhere.

MRS. NUDD (*as she plays Checkers*): Good for you, darling. Good for you.

MR. NUDD (*stepping out of the family circle; to audience*): It had begun to blow outside, and the house creaked gently, like a hull when the wind takes up the sail. (*He surveys his family*) The room with the people in it looked enduring and secure, though in the morning they would all be gone.

CHADDY (*making several jumps in checkers*): Crown me,
Mother. Crown me king.

MRS. NUDD: Oh Chaddy, you were always so good at
games . . .

(*Slow fade on all. The end.*)

12/98